AF256370

Just Below the Surface

An Initial Collection of 100 Poems

David Michaud

Copyright © 2024 by David Michaud

All Rights Reserved. No part of this publication may be reproduced, distributed, or transmitted in any form or by any means without the prior written permission of the publisher.

E-mail: davidmichaud@shaw.ca

Michaud, David , 1972-

Just Below the Surface
An Initial Collection of 100 Poems
ISBN: 978-1-7382900-1-7

For the memory of Leonard Cohen, whom I understand had empathy for everyone who was going through something. My 2010 discovery of my fellow Montrealer as a person and an artist shaped the course of my life. This collection is my attempt to go below the surface of things, like I understand L.C. did.

CONTENTS

VENERATION INSPIRING VOICE
{Inspired by Charles Baudelaire's poem
titled 'Remords Posthume'} [1]

At the bottom of the mountain, under the cross,
And while you have nothing for a pencil or pad,
But your long fingernails writing on muddy side walls.

When small rocks placed on your tombstone, affirming
conventions, and weighing down on your emaciated
body, work their way slowly,
Trying to stop your soul's search for meaning,
Attempting to prevent your mind and body from
continuing the disciplined task.

The same tomb entrusted with souls of past poets,
(Because the tomb always understands the journey is
what matters, it keeps poets alive indefinitely,)
Provides darkness to entice such creative types to rest.
The night no longer for living.

You say: << What do you use, imperfect poet, to fool
readers into believing you don't care whether they like
your writing? >>
-And the worms feast on your skin, like a shyness.
<<And what devices do you use to convince strangers
your writing is funny rather than Mourne? >>, I hear you
ask softly.

I respond that the vermin feast on my skin as much as
yours,
Also having been eaten alive long ago, in adolescence.
And I feast on your soul, nourished to sustain the effort.

All the while slowly abandoning your influence,
Replacing it with my own prophesy,
As even poets of modest talent are wont to do.

BEAST
{In the spirit of Charles Baudelaire}

I have not been okay since, Beast!
A wretched nightmare travelling swiftly.
Caravans carrying our hearts,
Encased in glass like Brother Andre,
Set off in different directions,
Yours to freedom offered by the Okanagan desert.

O despair! O despair! Time passes slowly in these new
locales,
In the darkness of catacombs,
On banks of sorrow-filled shores,
My soul obscured and you, now the enemy,
Gnawing at my hardened heart from afar.

But light inevitably shines through,
For there is a crack in everything,
My soul reassures me,
Someone beautiful waits nearby,
-Blond hair, subtle breasts visible through a white lace
dress.

I fear I will reach for her,
But will have to sit and rest until I eventually fall asleep.
Then I'll awaken to the feel of her behind me,
Running benevolent fingers through my hair.

GRANDEUR OF WAR
{In the spirit of Walt Whitman}

Returning upon my poems,
I consider wars waged and celebrated,
And my tendency to avoid conflict.
Where do I stand?
I too celebrate battles hard fought.

Yes, I also sing of war,
The greatest and longest lasting,
Waged in this book.
I jostle with mediocrity, lack of focus,
And fear the shame lurking in my mind's shadows.

I chant songs of battle,
And hope to be a brave soldier,
Capable of enjoying quiet sunrises at home,
Together with my beloved,
Before I lay breathless within earth and clay.

BEATNIK

{In the spirit of Ginsberg. To be sung while hitting two sticks together and counting "one-two, one-two" in your head.}

Don't be! Don't be! Don't be!
Don't be! Don't be! Don't be!
Don't wear that, not black
Always be clean, don't say what you mean

Don't be! Don't be! Don't be!
Don't be! Don't be! Don't be!
Don't joke like that, not funny
Always the latest fads, focus on all but the self

Don't be! Don't be! Don't be!
Don't be! Don't be! Don't be!
Don't go out, or you'll cheat
Always at home, late to sleep

Don't be! Don't be! Don't be!
Don't be! Don't be! Don't be!
No vacation, no dog
Yes to debt and keeping up

Don't be! Don't be! Don't be!
Don't be! Don't be! Don't be!
No career you'll love
No art, no poetry

THE INTERVIEW
{In the spirit of Charles Bukowski}

Sitting at CBC radio headquarters, across from Glen Gould's piano. Here it comes, the same boring question.

"Who are your poetic influences?"

"Do you really want to know?"

"Ask my dad. He's sitting right there. He's the reason I write poetry."

"Dad, you heard your son. Grab the headphones, please. Who are your poetic influences?"

"F.U., that's who. See it rhymes!"

"Let me guess, Charles Bukowski?"

"Pretty good. I thought you were a chump, but you are okay, man."

They went to commercial, and the producer ran in. "This is public radio. You can't say that."

"If its public can't I say anything I want because you can't censor the public? Put me back on, I'll be good."

"Would you explain your influence on your son's poetry?"

"That's what I just did. I've taught him to ignore
everyone, even his inner critic, for the sake of his art. I'll
let you continue without me. Peace out."

"What do you think?" the interviewer asked.

"My dad's authentic, and not boring. Maybe one day I
can be like him."

"He certainly is colourful."

"Speaking seriously, he is gentle and kind. He cares very
much what people think of him."

"Bukowski or your father?"

IT JUST IS, I SAID

One hundred thousand down
Men and women under stress
The war within always raging
Dead long before bomb shells land

Some feel lost
Scared of being deserted
Worried their food and rounds will be taken
By the powers that be

One amongst them stands out
Calm emanating
He thinks of home
Surrounded by the hot sun and cool mountain rivers

Nurturing his fears
Like a toddler who skimmed their knee
While others stop and sleep
Plans, rests, and continues to move forward

Elation
Yet the same familiar sense of peace
When he steps off the plane
And sees his family waiting for him

He has been home the whole time
He never left
They ask if it was hard
And he replies that war is senseless but inevitable

GARDEN OASIS

the tortoise was quote/unquote rescued at age 25
escaped first at the age of 26 and then again at 102
Why?
to find a mate
or are you asking why the turtle's minders trapped it in
the garden?
Why does anyone do anything?

ISHIN-DENSIN

Standing on a fairground
I wanted to escape to the banks of the river
A Buddhist Monk stood on a landing above
He continued his practice
Venerable Sir didn't seem to notice me
I wished I could be more like him

I entered the water
Let the canoe drift
Left the oars on the shoreline
got batted around
then returned to the calm stream
where water flowed slowly

PAST LOVES

<< Last month I dreamt of you.
I awoke to feel my blood
rushing through
and spasming my heart.

C'était le mois dernier quand j'ai rêvé de toi.
Mon cher, dis-moi ton nom
Pour que je puisse t'effacer
De ma mémoire.>>

GETTING BY

I've had an alluring but fleeting glimpse,
And what I've seen you may also have seen,
An escape to ephemeral calmness,
Where one returns to water of life's spring,
And benevolence and contentment flow.

My home straddles desert and waterway,
I would walk alone in hot, vast deserts,
If not for the company of kind whores,
Those who welcomed me inside graciously,
And bathed me in my soul's sandy mirage.

ADHD

I am a bee or a squirrel in the world,
Something you don't understand.

I'm off on my own,
Doing what I do.

A MIRRORED KISS

A kiss, just like this…
Smack on a mirrored glass.
Too literal. I'll try again.

A kiss, just like this…
Gently touching your wet lips.
Wait, I sense coldness from you.

A mirrored kiss, gentle as it is.
You and I in sync,
touching tenderly.

Now I should die,
Before this moment ends.
And I return to loneliness.

RETURNING TO [THE SIMPLE] LIFE

A small sparrow flies around a mountain corner,
Quickly in between Banff's mountainous valley.
Leaving night behind, rushing toward the light.
His flock pushing forward, no turning back.

Another bird joins him, a female robin.
An uncommon partnership, but one which feels natural.
Two chirps in sync, pulled along by the stream.
Not flying away from darkness, but instinctually moving
toward light.

They arrive and land on a twig.
Standing with the top of the sun's light slowly revealing
itself.
Enclosed by overhanging trees covered in snow.
They rest until called upon by instinct to head off.

The two leave in different directions,
Then cold dawn confronts him.
Tired and hungry, but at peace,
A new start awaits, minutes away now.

He is not the leader,
Although his confidence is high.
Why does he keep flying?
What else would he do?

Besides, it's more than flying!
An inward call to move toward the light.
He has spent days trying to find solace,
And there still is hope.

Now he believes he can change.
He dives downward, away from the flock.
But only so far as to be out of sight.
He feels brave and cherishes the adventure.

He changed, but quickly returned.
How often that happens!
After all, there is safety in numbers, and all that jazz.
Comfort arrives as frost melts and the sun rises.

The wind has died down and effort is required.
Now he flies without questioning why.
Enjoying the familiar sky, next to his fellow friends.
All is right in his little world, despite the chaos below.

TRIEZE ANS ET TOUT SEUL AU CENTRE-VILLE

La rue Ste. Catherine est plat,
Mais elle descend rapidement une fois que vous passez le
magasin de la Baie D'Hudson, après le Square Phillips.

J'ai aimé assister chez McDonalds,
Proche du quartier rouge ce qui est toujours intéressant.

Le restaurant Montréal Pool Room ou La Belle Province,
Et mon ami Robbie, qui était le propriétaire d'un Dunkin
Donuts
Ou il a servi du café au dames du la nuit.

Achat de jeans Levi's pour $28 chez les juifs; ou
Des écouteurs électroniques des Indiens.
Sam the Record Man, Discus et Dutchies; et
Une performance par Billy Bragg au Foufounes
Electriques.
En tant qu'enfant atteint de TDAH, j'ai adore la
nouveauté, la varieté, les rues sales, les gens, et
surtout l'aventure.

THANK YOU

Thank you, Leonard Cohen,
For ever picking up a pen.
For writing every word,
In every song I heard.
And for poems which touched my soul,
Got me to dip below the surface.
And helped me know,
I am not alone in the way,
I write poetry every day.

ABANDONED

We were scared
He entered our house
And took the Child Away
-My father didn't move or speak

We waited helplessly
After a long period
A child from the orphanage slowly entered
-My mother didn't move or speak

We are taking action
I killed my father and mother
And have found my foster-sister who is anxious and cold
-We wander in search of my sister

NEVER TOO YOUNG

I was a blond-haired Roman Catholic,
growing up in a Jewish area of Montreal,
Following kids through yards, over fences and across
driveways,
An old lady with a thick Hungarian accent, my friend's
grandmother, stopped me and said,
"I am proud of this," as she pointed to numbers tattooed
on her arm.
I wondered if it was charcoal that could be rubbed off,
And then I resumed playing.

DOWN FILLED DREAMS

Somebody nice gave me a warm jacket
It has been a source of nothing but pain
I wish they would return and take it back
Rather be cold in the wet snow and rain

DANIELLE

Danielle, my Beatrice
Images of aesthetic beauty
In your portfolio

Your glare embraced
the depths of my soul
And overwhelmed me with love

We were 17 and innocent
Exchanging mutual attraction
During our exchanges

Thirty years later
the encounter determined the whole of eternity
And I have not been okay since

THE ECSTASY OF BEING ALIVE

Cornered soldier
Bruised boxer
Cancer patient
Criminal with cops outside the door
A new relationship
Being given money
Vibing to a new song
Vibing to an old song
Feeling small in nature
Holding hands of a new love

HOW MY LONGING SHOWS UP

Alone on Friday afternoon
Sunlit artist studio
Drinking tea
Moving slowly
Nowhere to be

Night arrives
Mixing colours with each stroke
Picture slowly taking shape
Adding colour to my darkness
A state of understanding some emotions

Napping when tired
Changing music to match mood
Snacking on fruit and pastries
Slowing down to enjoy doing nothing at all
Unable to avoid unwelcome thoughts

Then a return to activity
Thoughts wondering
Painting again when the mood stirs
The source of my courage unlocked
The spring of inspiration returned

Meandering outside
Eating fresh fruit
A butterfly flies near
Removing my clothes, sweating
Walking around some more

Enjoying odors from plants
Moods impressed and compressed by nature
The height of inspiration
Hard to contain now
Back to the canvas with my unique nomenclature

The moon the only light
Sitting in a lawn chair
Calm, and then a burst of energy
Confident to travel below the surface of things
A fleeting instance of not holding anything back

Peaceful
Artistry flowing
Words written with ease
Energy of symbols
My body doesn't ache

When I am done
I step back and stand next to white carnations
Not at all associated with death
I like what I see
Is it good, or are endorphins at the root of it?

Indeed it is good
I went to my garden studio before dusk
Slowed down
Traveled below the surface of things
And watered beautiful parts of myself.

STAY WITH ME

I drove you to the bus station
after we made love
one last time

darkness and closed bridges
the ice storm
you asked if you could stay with me a while

we returned to my place
the one we called home
sat and talked under blankets

a friendship rekindled
love blossomed like a spring flower
you asked if you could stay with me a while

now, laying in the hospital
each breath hurting
looking into the same accepting eyes

tears filling your eyes
the same voice I heard at the station
asking me if you could stay with me a while

A MOMENT WHICH HAS LASTED A LIFETIME

At 5:30 in the morning Nanny died peacefully in her
sleep.
I answered the call from the hospital.

Mom was sad, lying face down on the bed.
I saw the sun hide behind a cloud.

Since 1979 I have been trying to find the comfort Nanny
provided.
And so has my mother.

I am learning to care for, and be there for myself,
So that my soul can rest.

ELATION FOLLOWED BY DISAPPOINTMENT

I walked the pathway beside the Bow River
and saw a beautiful 20-something Asian woman
going nowhere in particular
peaceful mudra and a Buddhist tattoo on her arm
I admired her peaceful presence
But was disappointed I would not ask to join her practice.

I FALL IN LOVE WITH "HER" AGAIN

Bitterly hearing bells at noon downtown,
Denominations clanging in the round.
Joining forces, stalking, wanting a fight,
Waking my brain from a long dark cold night.

Alas! An angel's voice, the joyful sound.
Edges of the new clouds are soft and round.
-Pastel tattoos, lace, and body so tight.
Gentle soft benevolent hands, so slight.

Reoccurring voids of darkness abound,
I awaken and she cannot be found.
I cannot demonstrate my strength and might.
Or plead with her to show me what is right.

My familiar survival instincts found,
I return to the depths, death all around.
Then I see her, and our souls reunite.
I fall in love again, then she takes flight.

A few minutes pass without a sound.
I return to the depths, death all around.
Then I see her, and our souls reunite.
I fall in love again, then she takes flight.

PARC DU PORTUGAL

Sitting on a bench
In beautiful Parc du Portugal
Tiles stained with the dirt of time
Brown gazebo covered in tree buds
Thick August heat

I sit next to an old man
He doesn't say anything at first
Then he tells me he lives alone
But his kids visit for dinner on Sundays
And he has a girlfriend down the street

BOHEMIAN WOMAN

At the Sunalta c-train station
I first caught sight of your small upturned breasts
And saw on your wrist, tattoos of pastel pink and blue

I entered a dream-like station
long blond hair, the sweetest smile, undressed
You touched me, but I would never touch you

You left for the Greyhound station
Your essence firmly appressed
I let your essence imbue

364 DAYS TIL EASTER SUNDAY

I travelled far to rekindle the us
On arrival I felt love's imbalance
Our hearts battling a strong impedance

Abruptly standing watching my likeness
Falling into the depths of the sadness
through the cold catacombs into darkness

It was time to leave for home's loneliness
She was very cruel, why I cannot guess
Talking with another, my resemblance

Her coldness not at all of my likeness
I offered myself some benevolence
And drank the red wine of Dionysus

Didn't we just share the carnal and kiss
with the sun's heat sheltered by sheer fabrics
And our young tight flesh so hard to harness

My beloved dear reader, hear me confess
I was there standing watching my likeness
Falling into the depths of the sadness

That instant my feet had weight of ballast
I sighed and my fragile bones turned porous
I fainted but was still fully conscious

But Godly influence did still insist
The morning's ecstasy could but persist
And provide my soul with its sustenance

The bus station's infernal ugliness
Times Square Port Authority floor's a mess
Sad and ugly, everyone more or less

I'd have preferred to die in nothingness
but I exercised a bold persistence
I waited for help and lived aloneness

Eventually when I decided to look for help less
Appearing before me was Beatrice
Who walked with me in the dense wilderness

Then Beatrice decided to progress
Tiring from emotions she was amidst
As is all my cherished lovers' aptness

I long for love of a woman to bless
But I fear the icy-cold end of us
So I remain here in my cave's darkness

DESPAIR

I ran into you,
And you said I look sad.
I thought, "Am I sad, or do you want me to despair?"

Another time,
I saw you and you flippantly waved your hand at me.
That was the first time I believed it had ended.

Years later,
You looked tired and unhappy.
I felt bad for you, for both of us.

POETRY

Writing poetry is like an ant going about its business between sidewalk cracks. It is like small birds landing on an edge between grass and pavement in search of worms. A consistent routine. Not only after it rains or when hungry.
A poet is like an ant searching for a morsel, dehydrated worms almost stepped on, birds hopping around unhospitable ground before returning to the comfort of flight.
Most of us resemble ants, worms and birds. Going about our day the way instinct dictates.

COURAGE

Reader, which version do you like better?

<u>Courage (Version 1)</u>
I'll leave him for you, she said.
I wanted to demand she follow through
And show me love every day
-kind words, understanding, giving herself sexually.
I said, I do want that.

<u>Courage (Version 2)</u>
I'll leave him for you, she said.
I can't yet, I said.
She got up, hugged me, and left.
I've resented her for not waiting for me
But in her wisdom, she knew I would never be with her.

<u>Courage (Version 3)</u>
I'll leave him for you, she said.
And I for you, I said.

GREAT CLIPS

Not me, the other fat hippy.
The one who cuts my hair,
coughs on my neck,
and sways rather than walks.

Over pants, a bohemian skirt,
Canvas shoes.
Cuts and styles,
Leaving my hair the perfect length.

Screw the Asian destroyer,
The arguing Croat,
The Egyptian lover of aftershave,
or the old Italian on Ste. Catherine's who cut Jean
Beliveau's hair.

Like one's mind visiting a transient nymph,
The other sickly, frumpy hippy
lifts my spirits,
and reminds me how I felt in my youth.

I WANT TO KNOW THE REAL YOU

Trying to be more self-absorbed, like a wild animal in the
forest.
Simply, reality everywhere.
Eat, then eat some more. Sleep, fight, eat, mate, and play.
Existing in a world without a notion of time.

I've placed blinders on my eyes to guard your beauty.
For the good of both of us.
Mindful separation cleared my vision and led to
acceptance.
Like Psykhe reunited with Eros, I am energized by
having caught a brief glimpse of your soul.

CALM ELUDES MY SOUL

Using a flimsy butterfly net
          to catch tiny crayfish
in a brook with fresh running water
My scurrying motion back and forth
              made the water murky
and I didn't catch anything

PARADISE LOST
*{Based on the poem entitled "Moesta et Errabunda" by
Charles Baudelaire in <u>Les Fleurs du Mal</u>.}*

Tell me, does your heart sometimes travel back, dear ?
Far from desolate prairies and the mundane,
Toward dirty cities bustling with energy,
Energetic, fast, large, confident it will outlast us ?
Tell me, does your heart sometimes travel back, dear ?

Take me, train ! Remove me, bus !
Far ! Far ! My heart remains frozen on the university's
cobblestone stairs !
Is it true your icy heart remains sad rather than kind ?
Are remorse's near crimes of the hearts sufferings ?
Take me, train ! Remove me, bus !

How you are far, perfumed lover !
Where youth was love, joy, and potential,
Tight bodies entwined without shame,
In the voluptuousness, pure hearts melded.
How you are far, perfumed lover !

Innocent paradise lost, sadness and longing replacing
pleasures,
Could we remember with desirous cries,
And hold each other again after bathing,
Feeling fulfilled when it comes to matters of the heart ?
Innocent paradise lost, sadness and longing replacing
pleasures.

HESITATION

When a visit from my dark passenger
creates moments when my fragile courage pisses the bed
and leaves,
As it is wont to do when my soul cries and laments my
decision to leave,
I become overcome with worry I will miss the two shades
of green leaves,
And small yellow flowers on my linden tree before nature
prompts them to also leave.

REALITY IN RELATIONSHIP

Stranger, let's live a lifetime in silence with separateness
sublime
As we lay naked with my head on the spot just above
your breast
Supressing worry our love will cease
Able to taste all the moment's flavours

Together we will climb quickly to the apex
And when the sky turns dark and a storm rolls in
I'll offer you my bones to craft a sled
And my blood to lay in front of you so you can glide to
safety

I will undertake a challenging trek home
Dying many times but waking stronger
Until one day I will saunter to where you are
As you tend your garden dressed in white lace

Stranger, lets get to know each other at the core
And live a lifetime together
In moments interrupted by silence
Absent worry that we will cease being

CANDOUR

I visited the dog park again,
Hoping to see the stranger,
Benny the Cockapoo's owner.

I went early,
Then at lunch,
And then again during sunset.

One time, during mid-afternoon,
Someone called for Benny,
But it was a guy's voice.

I lamented my fate.
Like Baudelaire and Cohen had before,
I thought about how all the beautiful women were taken.

And because I like to write poetry,
The 20 minutes spent thinking that were more enjoyable,
Then if I had chatted with Benny's owner.

And writing this down now,
I expose my attempt at humour,
But fear I only expose my weirdness.

PERISTERA

While we stared out the window on a hot summer
morning,
Past our view of couples arguing and strangers honking at
each other,
We saw a dove in the distance flying away with a fresh
cut olive leaf.

Satan's stance at our cherished bedside wasn't noticed,
So he implored you to ignore me and to then take leave.
You battled but acquiescence was inevitable.

Beelzebub romanticized my recollection of your
goodness.
So much so that I was frozen in place by your memory.
I remained in that place until a guide jabbed at my calf
and forced a step.

I moved slowly through cold landscapes, swamps, and
deep prairie fescue.
When alone again, I stood frozen.
Having fallen further than before.

After a time, I saw a firefly bring light in.
My soul had no choice but to limp slowly towards the
light.
Then while resting, I felt Beatrice running benevolent
fingers though my hair.

I awakened in a field of fresh smelling grass, a stream,
butterflies, and an orchard with fresh fruit.

AS WHEN I WAS 5 YEARS OLD

My father encouraged my kids
And I saw their eyes gush blood
His continued applause was deafening
Until he pierced his finger deep into their socket

I pushed my head into my pillow
Pounded the sheets in frustration
Closed my fists as tight as they would go
And cried.

REALITY ABOUT LEONARD AND I?

I'm thinking I shouldn't meet Leonard Cohen
while in Montreal,
since I may not like him.

I do very much like the notion of him,
but would likely be disappointed
by his ordinariness, or perhaps that he can be a real
asshole.

Or maybe I'd have to conclude
he is a great man,
and I am a boring, selfish jerk.

CHANGE

I threw a stick in the water
From a grassy ledge 15 feet above
And decided to follow it down river

It moved quickly at first
And I walked in tow
Until the stick stopped moving

Currents moved it from side to side
Then back to front
I paused and wrote something down

When I looked up
The current's ripples had pushed the stick
Slowly and steadily downstream

Nature's waves nudge me forward as well
But, unlike the stick, I moved opposite the waves
And impeded my own progress

SILENCE

Available to young and old, and those in between,
Not fragile or fleeting,
A rare thing under our control.

A source of great strength,
A powerful scream and benevolent comforter.
A sibling of nature, exertion, clarity, and wisdom.

A place of retreat when sad, angry, insecure, or anxious.
An effective container for one's emotions.
It never abandons.

A bridge over the large gorge within each of us,
Where echoes of emotions get lost and cannot be
recalled,
In time it returns to us that which was lost.

IT'S NOT YOU, IT'S ME

Like a habitual, impulsive criminal lamenting inevitable
incarceration,
I acted serious, lied, and hurt you in the process.
We both know I've had no intention of staying with you
forever,
But selfishly, it felt too good to stop.
Please don't take it personally,
I don't want anybody as a partner.
I've recently come to understand I only want
companionship.

HOW CAN IT BE?

You act like
You've forgotten our past.
From the heart,
We should talk.

You've forgotten our past.
We should talk.
Oblivion after drinking from the river Lethe,
You don't recall anything.

We should talk.
You don't recall anything.
Time doesn't erase memories,
Not even names of people we knew.

You don't recall anything,
Not even names of people we knew.
Your stance blunts my tongue, hobbles me,
And prevents you from lamenting our death.

HAVE YOU TRAVELED TO FAMILIAR PLACES?

Have you traveled to familiar places time and again, in
your dreams?
In my case, all are near water and dense lush trees while
on vacation.
Somewhere along the banks, evidence of a murder I
committed,
Remains untouched in a cave.
I worry others will discover my secret,
As we fly over the area.

GRACEFUL START

I am at my best on Saturday morning.
When I awake before dawn
Full of energy and a clear head
I clean my soul while cleaning the floors

I feed myself before preparing breakfast
Such activities nourish my soul
And provide me with an attitude of grace
With which to face the day

MENTAL ORDER

Today I saw a man walking with a limp
and half his face shaved,
like Dionysus' man-womanishness.
What surprised me was that
the side his beard was on
was opposite that of his gimp leg.
I guess his sense of order
Is different than mine.

HEADED TO THE PEN

I just left
the courthouse shackled
peace overtook my soul
you and the kids are destitute
but free from the monster I've become
from in here I can't hurt you anymore
joy for the first time in my pathetic life

KIND WOMAN GUARDING THE ENTRANCE

I was frenzied, nervous about what lay inside.
You also looked anxious, so I started a conversation.
I knew right away that you were kind,
And for the first time I appreciated and welcomed it.
You let me in, despite the long line
And you nervously touched my arm.
I felt sought after and my confidence soared.
That felt great, given how I had been feeling.
I keep the memory of you pure,
And it feels good to respect you since that is what you
deserve.

P.K.'s INTEGRITY

I envy how P.K. Subban is comfortable in his own skin.
His team, fans, and society ostracized him for it.
But he plays too well to care.
He shouted to the Bruins that he would win,
And then won.

OLD GUYS OUT FOR THE NIGHT

"Okay guys, tonight is going to be epic. Here's the plan –
Seven bars, one drink at each bar. Crazy, right?"
The three of them hadn't been out in months.
"Let's make it even more fun," Stephen said. "We'll each
pick personas to tell the girls we meet."
"I'm gonna be a former CFL player named Dax. No last
name, just Dax. During the off-season I'm a rodeo
clown."
Stephen gleamed. "Brilliant! Except you are 5 foot 7 and
120 pounds. Nobody will believe you played football.
I'm gonna be a millionaire named Steve-O, with houses
in Calgary and Vancouver. I'll tell them I own Cowboys
Casino." Steve embraced his new personality and smiled
arrogantly.
"And you, Sam?"
"I'm going to tell people I host the "Sam-pede" every
year, and that hundreds of people come to my rodeo. It
takes place a week before the Stampede. I'll have to
explain I'm not a rodeo cowboy, just the organizer. Oh
yeah, and I'll tell every couple I meet that they are
beautiful specimens." Tonight, I'm on the search for the
king and queen of Calgary. Sam spoke with a mild lisp.
"That's ridiculous." Steve-O slammed back a shot and
said, "Well, one arrogant millionaire, a pint-sized football
player, and an insecure 'non-bronco-bucking' 60-year-old
wearing a tweed trench coat. We could have been
anything and that's where we landed. Let's go out and
have some fun."

TO KISS MY SPOT ON YOUR CHEST

Your soul remains mingled with mine,
Despite the passage of time.
The past is done,
But I would like to hold you near.

I dwell on our lost love,
Not out of regret for things not done.
For the acceptance you offered,
Which fulfilled my longing.

Our end, at your discretion,
Showcased your admirable resolve.
Like a prisoner with a lifetime bid,
I crave to be released from this hell.

All is an effort.
Will it always be?

A HIPPY NOTION OF LOVE

As I get older, I am comfortable with the notion of living
alone.
Please feel free to leave.
I do love you very much, so I do hope you will stay.

I now feel closer to you and am committed to the
unromantic notion of "us."
So please don't step onto that train, run crying from a
church, or turn the car around to return to me.

It feels healthier, being an equal free-willed participant in
this relationship.
Everyday is an opportunity to choose to love you,
And for you to love me.

VACATION BACK HOME

Connectedness, less loneliness.
Acceptance, more relaxation.
Relaxed shoulders, rested mind.
Unrushed, feeling at home.

I want to give,
Understand, listen, and help.
Guide and play,
Be a good uncle, brother, son, and friend.

Cherish time with my parents,
Reconnect with my sister and brother,
Sister-in-law and brother-in-law.
Bullshit with my friends.

Wander, lounge, sit and drink,
Write, draw, sit and think.
Be both selfish and selfless,
Lazy and energetic.

I'd like to chat with a stranger over coffee,
And feel energized afterward.
Visit aging aunts and uncles,
Cherishing the time and opportunity.
Most of all,
I want to think and act positive,
Without any judgement, anger, or impatience.
For my soul and for the enjoyment of those around me.

INSECURITY IN RELATIONSHIPS

In conversation I said what I didn't mean.
Because I thought it was what you needed to hear
For you to like me.

It was exhausting because I was not being my authentic
self.
And the times I was authentic, feedback was that I talked
too much.
Which is why I enjoy writing, where only I critique
myself.

THE GREAT WAR

My training did not prepare me
For the horrors that would lie ahead.
The send off made me excited to be a hero,
Ready for the voyage.

Every soldier would like more armor
After realizing during battle
That he is naked and no longer protected
By the chain-armor blanket he brought from home.

The incendiary explosiveness of the barbs
And the silence and futility of my ineffective
counterstrike
have caused me to no longer attack with vigor.
My training did not prepare me.

I became a pacifist and no longer raised arms.
Alone, I hunkered in my bunker.
Shivering and alone
Despite being surrounded by my peers.

Trying to find courage to move.
Everyone else was firing at will.
Tying to kill the other.
I've turned into myself.

Having arrived home,
I sit content in the safety of my home.
In front of a warm fire
While a storm rages outside and people are being killed.

HUMILITY

There is great value in being able to separate
Shame resulting from actions of others
From that resulting from our own brokenness

IT'S OVER

I long to return to past lovers.
Most of them at least.
Part of me knows return is not possible.
That women have (likely) moved on.
I feel sadness at my core.
It must be included as one factor at the root of my
unhappiness.

ANTI-ABORTION LAWS IN 2022

U.S. babies say thank you.
Until their mother commits suicide,
And they both die.

MODERNITY

Porn is ecstasy and misogyny,
Wrapped together.
For one to be compassionate,
And altruistic in their actions,
They must avoid the trap of the mind,
And balance pureness of thought and deed.
Something I've been lousy at.

AN ALLEYWAY IN CÔTE ST-PAUL

Sitting on my balcony
I notice my neighbour's laundry hanging

I let the thin dog
Eat out of my garbage

Children can be heard
Playing street hockey in the alleyway

I see the bicycle
Scurrying away from the depanneur

I sit alone
And watch life taking place

COMMITMENT

I say to myself, "You bitch! I want you to leave
immediately. Get out of my sight."
But I know that, for my own health, I must caress you,
And spend days joined at your hip.
I push my sadness and disappointment below the surface,
Where it simmers.
My outside appearance is good, but I am dying inside.
To make matters worse, the other found and closed my
lone escape route.
So I remain trapped.
Two months have passed, and the judge remains frozen
with gavel in hand.
I want to disobey the court and rush the bench to lower
her hand.
Patience is required, because any action other than loving
tenderness to you will alert security forces and result in
my banishment to the penitentiary.
So, I recommit. Make you some tea with a little milk, the
way you like it,
Peel fruit and put my arms around you lovingly.
I do enjoy when you let out your half-smile, attempting to
hide your fear and disappointment.
As I sit with you, I wait patiently until the day you
disappear,
So I can leave this place and check into the Super 8 motel
With only my clothes on my back. Then maybe I will
stop worrying.

MY PARTICULAR ADDICTION

Once in a while I long to be with a beautiful woman
Who has been broken to sustenance
As if the darkest recesses of my soul are illuminated
By the brightness of their humility and beauty.

But I have learned such light only penetrates the surface.
It is grabbed by the dark shadow and pulled below,
Into a darkness so strong it casts a slow-moving eclipse
On all who try to balance a square life
With ecstatic experience.

SHAMBLES

She said, "I can't believe I let you fuck me."

I could tell she meant it.
I told her I'd still like to hang out as friends.

She couldn't remember why she was ready to leave her
family,
Or how she was consumed with everything I offered.
She had been broken, looking for me to provide things
her husband was unable to.

When she offered to leave everything for me,
I said I had to stay put.
As if a light switch activated, she recommitted to her
husband.

The next time she saw me,
I looked tired and ugly.
At least that's how I felt.

Forces didn't stop working.
She continued longing for something more,
And I still seek love from a beautiful, benevolent woman.

RESTING PLACE

A few of my uncles made it clear
They didn't want public notice or a funeral when they
died.
I wonder where that stems from.
Regardless, I feel the same.
It makes me wonder if it's part of our DNA,
Or if it's the experience of our lives,
And those of our ancestors.

I crave solitude while I'm alive,
So I definitely want to be alone after I die.
I watched a movie and asked myself
What the characters were doing carrying
A dead body down the mountain.
I can think of nothing better than remaining
Alone near the mountain top for eternity.

The opposite would be true
If I remained dead at the foot of the mountain
And had to remain amongst humanity
And hear conversations of hikers walking by.

THE SQUALL OF DESPAIR

You say summer will come after the smoke clears
And I will leave the darkness of this tunnel
And temporarily be blinded by the sun's brightness
Before viewing God's wondrous creation

Then, and only then
Will I find the strength to welcome the sun each morning
And find courage to fall in love again
That seems so far away right now

Until the day comes
I will continue moving slowly
I'll lament everything
As I begrudgingly complete tasks

They tell me to look at the positive side
Well, I've returned to myself
I sit, think, and then breath… like you told me to do
I've taken the first step on the long trip home

IMPERMANENCE OF LOVE

When I was with you
laying my head on my spot
in the middle of your chest,
just above your boobs,
I felt joy mixed with fear.

Now, years later,
my fear that those moments would end
has become reality.

TRANQUILITY IS NOT IN THE CARDS

My mind instilled with energy of Bia,
A force off the charts like Pollock in his prime,
A methhead on a bender,
Or a concert drummer beating rhythmically.
All speaking to me in sequence.

My head has the bustle of a New York subway.
An overwhelming noise which feels like home.
The ability to sleep on a dirty train platform.
Finding the constant sensations comfortable.
All I've ever known.

Will I have to wait until I get old?
When my brain's nerve-endings fade,
Or otherwise connect to one another?
For my mind to get a break?
All up to my body only.

I have rare glimpses of peace.
When barefoot on grass or dirt, when sleeping,
When showering and during the strain of a last
weightlifting set
But such times are few and far between
-All I do is aimed at achieving quiet in my head.

OPIATE

Saturday afternoon
Birds chirping
But I'm not singing their tune

Alone in my room
Under the sheets
Pleasure followed by guilt

An opportunity is spotted
I put on an old song
And doze off in peace

The ecstasy comes in stages
A natural effect of opiates
In and out of sleep, at peace for now

DAD

A car hit him straight on
And he walked away unscathed
Not because he is Superman
It is due to the barriers erected

He wasn't the same afterwards
He hid a limp
And locked his kids inside
For fear they'd be hurt as badly

PERSIAN GIRL

The work week finally ended.
I've run right over to you.
It's time to abandon earthy reality.

I want to spend the evening with you.
together as friends.
The weekend? Forever perhaps?

You want me to give you all my attention.
To be man enough to fulfill your needs.
I selfishly try to enter your heart anyway.

DEHUMANIZATION

I was a grey ghost, gaunt as van Gogh's subjects.
Crowds rushed by mindlessly looking at their cellphones,
Wearing blouses of reds, yellows, and greens.

The blue pants and shirt of the paramedic,
Leaning full weight on my chest,
As I was wheeled along the c-train platform.

You kept your headphones in and punched your ticket home.
But you didn't even glance over at me,
During the moment I've anticipated since first learning I would die.

I AM FRAGILE, SO PLEASE LOVE ME

I felt elation, acceptance, and happiness,
When you expressed a desire to be with me.

And each time I saw you naked,
I felt an indescribable joy.

I worried when you pulled away,
As it confirmed the negative, defeatist, self-loathing part
of myself.

I felt defeat when your sensual nature became dominated
by your mind.
And you closed both your mind and soul to me.

LEAVES FALLING

Fall in Alberta.
Walking in a forest.
A mix of dark green and half-green/half-yellow leaves.

A handful of leaves fall.
Dust flies up from the path into my eyes.
White pollen floats through the air.

I get the urge to tug at a thin branch.
Trying to make the leaves fall.
To no avail since nature is in control.

Some leaves are not ready to fall,
While others fall, far from their original position,
Due to the slightest of winds.

During fall,
I listen to classical music,
And feel a call to be outside appreciating nature.

FRUIT FLIES

Phantom eyebrow Ti-Fighters,
Endless searching for their nurturing bosom.
A test of will.

Alas, the discovery is shocking,
Fearfully returning the life source to nature,
Before its travel to the death camp.

Immediate calm,
Like after labour, sex, or swimming.
I kind of miss the pests.

THOUGHTS ON A HOT SUMMER NIGHT

A large black fly
Helmet with antennae
Lands on a glass balcony
And he becomes mindless
Unable to do anything
For that instant
Other than stick to the glass
Then he remembers he can fly
And off he goes

MOOD AND PERCEPTION OF THINGS

After a late night
the morning and a tired state
Can sometimes bring a critical eye
to my surroundings
-Apartment walls seem dirty from a certain angle.
-Lives of my friends can seem petty and unattractive.

EGO AND ENVY

An old man walking slowly
Observes young people walking towards him.
An average looking girl bristles with confidence.
"I envy her." he thinks to himself.
"Her confidence is amazing, given she is otherwise
average."

A DREAM

After many years,
A mountain has changed.
It is now my job to erect a sign,
Advising people.

Instead of meeting the expectation,
That the sign be clear,
I scribble the information messily.
And I don't feel bad about it.

FRAGILE

Picking up on her accepting vibe,
he loosens up and decides to stay with her.
He has work left to do still,
but now he is confident.
She won't reject him.
Fast forward two days and it has ended.
How often that happens.

TIME DOESN'T ALWAYS HEAL

You can act like
Everything is okay.
We should talk.
From the heart.
Time doesn't heal everything.

Twenty years passed.
Remnants of our love remains.
I've changed in that I don't want you,
But I'm mad you don't recall anything.
Time shouldn't erase memories. It should only fade them.

SOMETHING HAS CHANGED

Did I notice anything different?
I should have said no, definitively.
But instead, my yes was undifferentiated.

I saw lips meshing with the neck, and
hands making the touchdown signal,
the shoulder shrug, eyebrows making eyes bug out.

I saw it many times.
By the third time,
I accepted that the pattern had changed…
and it bothered me.

Two weeks later,
chemicals stopped movement.
Now I am fine,
Look at me as I bite my nails,
Watch three seasons of a Netflix series,
And fantasize about sex.

'TIS ME LOOKING BACK

'Tis a cruel reality
I can't go back;
Your beauty and grace
        Are out of reach;
No more of the acceptance you kindly offered
        And no loving touch.
Reflecting back on being loved,
        I long to return to your kiss.

I'll not leave you,
        I'll not move on;
Since your partner awaits
        Go sleep with him;
Thus in solitude I suffer
        Your image won't leave me;
Holding on to the hope
        We'll be together when old.

MUST HAVE SEEN A SPECIAL WOMAN

I had pep in my step,
Like Bo Jangles,
When Bo forgot how to sing the blues for an instant.
-Must have seen a special woman.

Accepting glance and small hands,
Riding the high for days,
Excited by many firsts.
-Must have seen a special woman.

It also happened once when I was going about my day,
And a tall beauty smiled at me,
And I smiled back.
-I've seen a special reflection of myself.

In that moment,
My soul was satisfied,
And I felt good about myself.
-I've seen a special reflection of myself.

SUDDENLY OLD

I think like a person who is still young,
my vessel is as a cancerous lung.
A thing that I never accepted ever,
that my life too will not last forever.
Suddenly God's scheduled time warp attack,
it has wrinkled my hand and curved my back.

Alone on my balcony I quiver,
And then enjoy the view of the river.
On LaSalle Boulevard should I bike or run,
bounding shirtless in the scorching summer sun?
Hanging out with friends and swimming in pools
Wasting away the days like fools?

I wish I could go back,
Run 15 kilometres, get hammered and have sex.

PROCESS

Dark,
The moth repetitively hits the window
Trial and error

I turn on a light
The moth stops trying
Slowly flies away aimlessly

I was the same way…

Dark
Trying, controlling, striving
Trial and error in my efforts to feel content

Now I've slowed
But still repetitively hit up against the window
Trying instinctually

AUTHENTICITY

When I was young
A breakup had meaning.
Now the onset has meaning
But the after-affect is short lived.

No more running at full speed
Instead, she's in and out of my thoughts
For a few weeks
Before I start to wonder if I even liked her.

I'm feeling like the only person
I will continue loving
Is a woman who will accept me
And spend time when I am being true and unfiltered.

OYAJI

My Japanese friend Shin (Shinjiro) called me a twenty-
year-old "oyaji."
Getting up early, enjoying flowers and leaves.

SINCE FIRST SEEING YOU NAKED

I cannot describe
Depths of my longing
Nor my elation
Your skin was so soft
Come back to my arms
Once and for always
I long for your smile

What's your name again?
I want to hold you
Nuzzle at your breasts
Use you for my soul
Come into my arms
Once and for always
Beautiful stranger

NEW LOVE... 5 SECONDS OLD IN FACT

I would like to meet you,
6 seconds ago a stranger,
Now my soulmate,
While we live our lives during the next 2 minutes.

Ideally, you and I won't talk,
As silence forms deeper connection,
And attempts to do the impossible,
By delaying our inevitable separation.

Our spiritual attraction,
Would prompt the physical,
To reach peaks only the two of us could summit.
And we'd remain alone at the apex,
Caring for one another's needs incessantly.

And when the day comes,
For the mother of all storms,
And we are covered in rain, snow, and cold,
I'd offer my bones to craft a sled,
And my skin to gloss the bottom.
You'd spread my blood in front of you,
As you'd escape to the safety below.

ACHE

The reality is that I walk alone, feeling lonely,
As much as I did when I was 5, 17, and 25.

The only things which have satisfied the ache in my soul
Has been company of a woman who is into me,
And very rare moments when I feel my poetry is good.

What do I want?

To be in a white dress shirt and tailored suit,
Sitting in a café,
Speaking easily with a beautiful woman.
She is into me, I am confident,
and we sit and drink tea for hours.

BANKS OF THE RIVER

As I stand on the rivers shore,
I notice two waves meeting each other,
One from the east and one from the west.
The two never becoming one another.

HOW MY LONELINESS SHOWS UP

At noon I was walking the avenue
Very much alone
Everyone else seemed to be laughing with someone
I heard a voice so beautiful
Smelled skin so fragrant
Bees strayed off their course
When my mind returned, she was gone
I had wanted her to notice me
I walked slowly
Waiting to fall in love with the next woman I saw.
At noon I was walking the avenue
Very much alone.

BOREDOM

Like bacteria, she passively stretches over every expanse,
Seeps into dark crevices along the path of least resistance,
Exhausting the few who try to avoid being overtaken.

The few times I've moved towards her alluring call,
My thoughts turned negative, and my notion of art was
purged,
I felt a surge in my organs and pushed towards old age.

The only chance one has is to dance, to get moving.
Others around will cast shadows when you do.
People love casting shame on ecstatic experiences.

As for me, my soul takes my hand and leads me to
society's underbelly,
As far as a square guy can travel,
And, for a time, I feel a strong positive energy.

When morning comes, I return to my vanilla life.
She fools my mind into thinking I am content with the
mundane.
Nonetheless I do feel recharged.

That is, until a few days pass and I again long for
experience.

ENJOYMENT

I've been at this temple a short time.
Exhaustion, beaten and spent.
-The most joy I've felt.

PRE-SCHOOLERS AND CRACKHEADS

They both ride their bike in deep snow,
And walk alone slowly with their heads down,
Pulling clothes behind them.
Their parents drive by asking if they are okay.
They are sleepy and late for appointments,
And both may pee their pants at any moment,
They get followed when they shop for fear that they will
shoplift,
And neither have the skills yet to navigate life.

PLAYING THE ODDS

"I will leave him for you," she said.

You engross me, he thought to himself.

Seeing tears forming in her eyes, he wanted to communicate his desire for her to always demonstrate love for him. Through kind words, patience, and giving herself sexually. He would give her the same in return. He kept it to himself.

Despite knowing he would never leave his wife for her, he said, "I do want that." While not a wise man, he knew that being truthful would have hastened their end.

His mistress would one day move on, but the effect of the mistruth on his esteem immediately set in motion an undercurrent in his soul which excited the devil.

Now inescapable, the realization of his meekness, lack of integrity, and aloneness haunted him incessantly. Those around him did not know, but he was tormented.

WRITTEN WITH LAUREN

When young
Planted with crooked stem
In front of the new home

The first few years
Only leaves
As flowers yet to develop

The tree blooms in late July
When the moon is full
And life seems most calm

The flowers fall
September bright moon
With clouds that surround it

It won't be long
Till the time comes to sleep
And energy is gathered for the job ahead

CANADA DIVIDED – ELECTION 2019

The Alberta Liquor & Gaming Commission liaison arrived. He was wearing a pin-striped suit, a red tie, and a small Liberal Party of Canada pin which he had forgotten to remove.

The doorbell rang, after a time, a well-dressed grey haired 50-year-old opened the door. He looked the man up and down.

"Do you actually support the communists?" he asked.

"I have the pleasure of notifying you that you've won 15.6 million in the lottery."

"Go to hell," the man said as he slammed the door in the liaison's face.

The lottery commission liaison reported back to Toronto. The clerk asked what the problem was. "It seems the man who won dehumanized me. Perhaps he had an attitude because his father taught him intolerance to differences, or maybe he is a sheep falling in lockstep with the views of his peers. His loss."

BIBLIOGRAPHY

1. Scarf, Francis

2012. Baudelaire *The Complete Verse*. London: Anvil
Press Poetry Ltd, p. 109.